J

# Arabians

## and Other Horses

Editor in Chief: Paul A. Kobasa
Supplementary Publications: Lisa Kwon, Christine Sullivan, Scott Thomas
Research: Mike Barr, Timothy J. Breslin, Cheryl Graham, Barbara Lightner, Loranne Shields
Graphics and Design: Kathy Creech, Sandra Dyrlund, Charlene Epple, Tom Evans
Permissions: Janet Peterson
Indexing: David Pofelski
Prepress and Manufacturing: Anne Dillon, Carma Fazio, Anne Fritzinger,  Steven Hueppchen,
    Tina Ramirez
Writer: Karen Ingebretsen

Special thanks to Daphne Levitas, Pat Parrish, and Cindy Stylianos for their helpful suggestions
and advice.

**For information about other World Book publications, visit our Web site at
http://www.worldbook.com or call 1-800-WORLDBK (967-5325).**

**For information about sales to schools and libraries, call 1-800-975-3250 (United States);
1-800-837-5365 (Canada).**

World Book, Inc.
233 N. Michigan Avenue
Chicago, IL 60601
U.S.A.

**Library of Congress Cataloging-in-Publication Data**

Arabians and other horses.
     p. cm. -- (World Book's animals of the world)
   Summary: "An introduction to Arabians and Other Horses, presented
in a highly illustrated, question and answer format. Features include
fun facts, glossary, resource list, index, and scientific
classification list"--Provided by publisher.
   Includes bibliographical references and index.
   ISBN-13: 978-0-7166-1331-2
   ISBN-10: 0-7166-1331-X
   1. Arabian horse--- Miscellanea--Juvenile literature.  2. Horses--
Miscellanea--Juvenile literature.  I. World Book, Inc.  II. Series.
SF293.A8A67 2007
636.1--dc22
                    2006017309

Printed in Malaysia
1 2 3 4 5 6 7 8 09 08 07 06

**Picture Acknowledgments:** Cover: © Mark J. Barrett; © Taxi/Getty Images; © Dennis MacDonald, PhotoEdit; © Barbara
Wright; Animals Animals.

© Arco/Alamy Images 35; © Juniors Bildarchiv/Alamy Images 4, 39, 51; © M Stock/Alamy Images 19; © Prenzel
Photo/Animals Animals 3, 15, 37; AP/Wide World 59; © Mark J. Barrett 7, 17, 23, 29, 31, 41, 53; © Colin Dutton,
SIME/4Corners Images 27; © Taxi/Getty Images 61; © Kim Houghton, Corbis 21; © Dennis MacDonald, PhotoEdit 55;
© Robert Maier, SIME/4Corners Images 43; © Yva Momatiuk & John Eastcott, Minden Pictures 5, 33, 49; © Carl & Ann
Purcell, Corbis 45; © Jason Smalley, Wildscape/Alamy Images 25; © Peter Weimann, Animals Animals 57; © Barbara Wright,
Animals Animals 5, 47.

**Illustrations:** WORLD BOOK illustrations by John Fleck 9, 13.

# Arabians

## and Other Horses

**World Book, Inc.**
a Scott Fetzer company
Chicago

# Contents

# What Is a Horse?

A horse is a large, four-legged animal with solid hoofs, a flowing mane, and a tail of long, coarse hair. Horses are herbivorous *(hur BIHV uhr uhs),* which means they eat grass or other plants, but no meat. Horses are also mammals—animals that feed their young with milk made by the mother.

Horses can be divided into three main groups: ponies, heavy horses, and light horses.

The first group—ponies—is made up of small horses that stand less than 58 inches (147 centimeters) high when fully grown.

The heavy-horse group includes horses used for farm work, pulling carriages, and general riding.

In the light-horse group are saddle horses, which are used for pleasure riding, ranch work, and racing. Arabians are a type of saddle horse in the light-horse group. The light-horse group also includes horses used for harness racing—a type of racing in which a horse pulls a driver in a light, two-wheeled cart.

An Arabian horse

# Why Can a Horse Run So Fast?

A horse is a beautiful and majestic animal that is well adapted for running. A horse has large muscles in the upper part of its legs that provide speed. Its long, thin legs give the horse a long stride.

A horse's feet are ideal for running. Each foot is a single, very strong toe. Only the tip of the toe, protected by the strong, curved hoof, touches the ground. The animal that was the ancestor of the horse had two additional toes. Those additional toes changed to bony strips that run from the top to midway down the cannon bone in the leg of a modern horse.

The fastest types of horses are quarter horses (see page 34) and thoroughbreds (see page 38). The quarter horse can run short distances faster than any other horse. It can run a quarter-mile (0.4 kilometer) in less than 21 seconds. The thoroughbred is faster at long distances. It can run a mile (1.6 kilometer) in 1 minute 33 seconds. By comparison, the fastest a human has ever run a mile in is 3 minutes, 43 seconds.

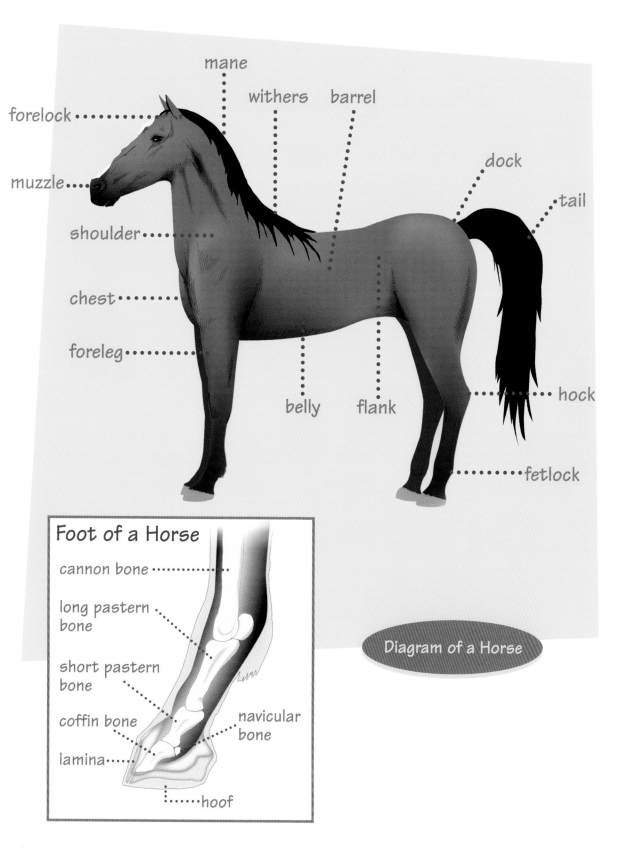

mane

withers

barrel

forelock

dock

tail

muzzle

shoulder

chest

foreleg

belly

flank

hock

fetlock

## Foot of a Horse

cannon bone

long pastern bone

short pastern bone

coffin bone

navicular bone

lamina

hoof

Diagram of a Horse

# What Are Arabians and Where Did They Come From?

Arabians are one of the oldest breeds of horses. A breed is a group of animals of the same species (kind) that has the same type of ancestors. Horses of all breeds have descended from wild horses that were tamed by humans thousands of years ago. There are more than 150 breeds of horses and ponies today.

The Arabian breed may date to before 3000 B.C. and was probably native to western Asia. No one knows for sure what the ancestors of the Arabian horse looked like. Some historians believe these ancestors were fine-boned animals that were no more than 48 inches (122 centimeters) tall at the top of the shoulders, which are called the withers (see page 9).

The Arabian horse is known for its strength and endurance, or staying power. Arabs developed this breed for use in the desert. For hundreds of years, breeders in many countries brought these horses from Arabia, an area that today is called the Arabian Peninsula. Horse breeders used the Arabian horses they imported to develop new breeds.

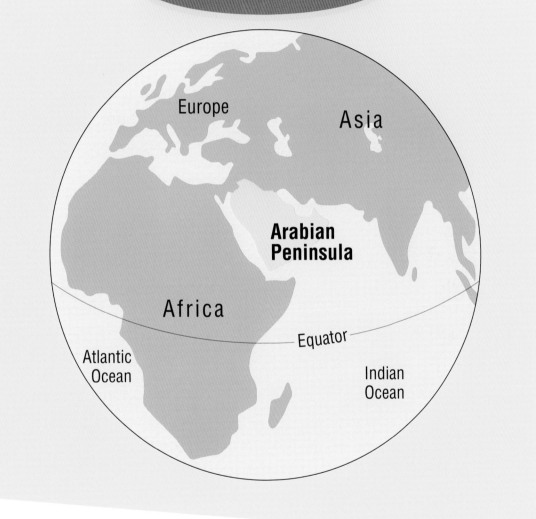

Map showing the peninsula where the Arabian developed

Europe

Asia

**Arabian
Peninsula**

Africa

Equator

Atlantic
Ocean

Indian
Ocean

# How Do Horses, Including Arabians, Measure Up?

Horses vary greatly in size.

The smallest breed of horse is the Falabella. Falabellas were originally bred in Argentina and are kept as pets. Falabellas measure around 30 inches (76 centimeters) high at the withers and may weigh as little as 70 pounds (32 kilograms).

When fully grown, ponies are less than 58 inches (147 centimeters) high at the withers. Most ponies weigh less than 800 pounds (360 kilograms).

The largest horse breed was developed in England. The shire draft horse can be more than 68 inches (173 centimeters) high at the withers and can weigh 2,000 pounds (910 kilograms) or more. Shires are among the strongest horses.

Most Arabians weigh somewhere between 850 and 1,000 pounds (between 390 and 450 kilograms) and are around 14 to 15 hands (56 to 60 inches, or 142 to 152 centimeters) high.

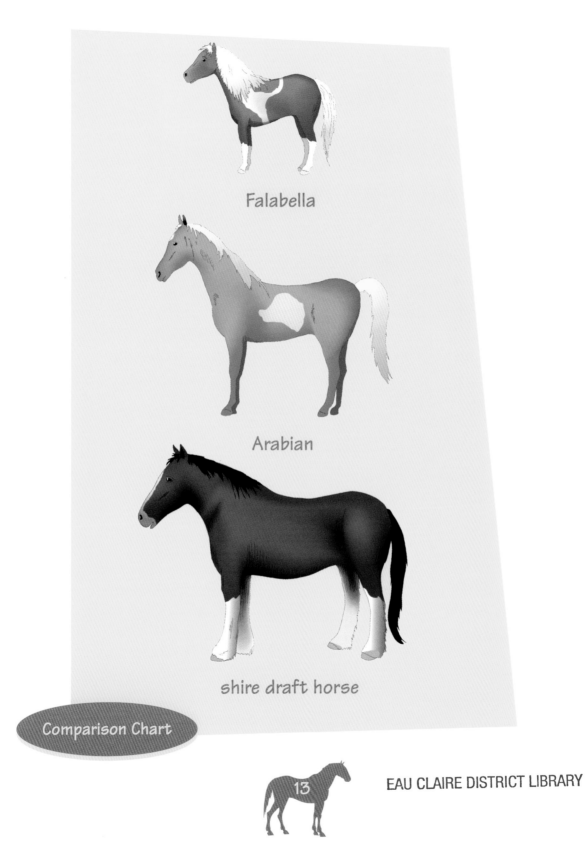

Falabella

Arabian

shire draft horse

Comparison Chart

# What Kind of Personality Might an Arabian Horse Have?

Most Arabian horses are loyal animals that strive to please the humans who care for them. Because Arabians were bred and raised in close contact with humans from earliest times, these horses have a great ability to bond with humans. Their affectionate nature makes them a good family horse.

Arabians also make great competitors in horse shows. They are known for their endurance, balance, agility, speed, and grace.

Just like horses of any other breed, each Arabian is different, with its own personality. You will find warm, mischievous, stand-offish, and affectionate Arabians. Some Arabians are easily startled, though others are not. Some have long attention spans, and others have short attention spans.

Getting to know a horse and its personality is one of the important responsibilities of an owner.

Arabians form close
bonds with people

15

# What Should You Look for When Choosing an Arabian Horse?

If you are buying a family horse, then the horse's personality and its overall appearance will be important. Do you like the horse's color, head, and expression? Do you feel an attraction to the horse? Does the horse have any bad habits?

Ask the owner or handler about the horse's health, and ask an adult to carefully examine the horse. During this exam, that adult should be concerned if any pain, fear, anger, sluggishness, or unusual sleepiness is sensed in the horse.

Ask about the horse's registration. Even if its registration is not important to you, it may be important to a future buyer should you decide to sell the horse.

Ask about the horse's training history. See how the horse performs with the owner or handler, then "test ride" the horse yourself.

16

Arabians are often chosen for shows and competitions

# What Is the Difference Between a Pasture, a Paddock, and a Stable?

A pasture is a fenced, grassy field or hillside on which horses can live and feed. A paddock is a smaller, enclosed field near a stable or house. A stable is a building fitted with stalls, where horses are kept. Most stables also have a storage area for feed and an area for tack—that is, saddles and other riding equipment.

A horse that lives without a stable needs a run-in shed for shelter from the hot sun and from inclement weather. A run-in shed is a rectangular shelter that has three sides enclosed and one side open. Such a shelter should be big enough to hold all the horses that use the pasture or paddock.

Each type of living place—pasture, paddock, or stable—has some advantages for the horses kept there. Most people choose where to keep their horses based on what is most practical.

Thoroughbreds in a paddock

# What Should a Stall Look Like?

A stall, which is an individual place for one horse in a stable, should measure at least 10 feet by 12 feet (3 meters by 3.5 meters). It should be light, dry, and well ventilated. If possible, the stall should have a window, which improves airflow. The door to the stall should be a Dutch door—a door that is divided horizontally. When the bottom half of this door is closed, the horse is still able to poke its head out of the top half of the door. The horse can see what is happening and interact with its stablemates (if it has any). This helps prevent the horse from becoming bored.

The best flooring for a stall is clay or finely ground cinders. But cement or wooden floors covered with rubber mats can be used.

Bedding can be made of such materials as wood shavings, sawdust, straw, or peat moss. It should be spread at least 1 foot (30 centimeters) thick. Although bedding is spread on the floor of a horse's stall, often a horse may sleep standing up. Its eyes will still be half-open as it stands, dozing.

A horse peering
through the top half of
its Dutch door

# How Do You Groom a Horse?

Grooming helps keep a horse's coat healthy and improves a horse's appearance. It is also an excellent way to check a horse for any cuts or irritations on its skin. Horses kept in a stable should be groomed daily with a body brush, a mane and tail comb, and a currycomb.

Rubbing a horse's coat with a currycomb brings dirt to the surface and gives the coat a healthy glow. Brushing removes dirt and dandruff. After brushing, a horse should be wiped down with a soft cloth.

A water brush and sponges are useful to have in your horse's basic grooming kit. When used wet, a water brush helps train the hairs of the tail and mane to lie flat. Sponges are used to wipe the horse's eyes, nostrils, and also around the dock, which is the thick, fleshy covering over the horse's tail bones at the top of its tail.

A horse's hoofs should be checked daily, as well.

A horse being groomed

23

# Why Does a Horse
# Need Shoes?

Shoes protect the feet of horses that run or work. Light shoes that weigh about 8 ounces (230 grams) and use only a few nails make the best shoes for most horses. Horses need new shoes every four to eight weeks, depending on how fast their shoes wear out and how fast their hoofs grow.

Tennessee walking horses (see page 34) wear shoes weighted in the toes to help them raise their feet high. Race horses wear very light shoes. Shoes for winter or for high mountain trails have grips to help keep the horse from slipping on ice or snow.

Most horseshoes are made of steel or aluminum. They are nailed to the horse's hoofs. A farrier, or blacksmith, does this type of work. When the shoe is nailed on properly, it does not hurt the horse. Hoofs are made of keratin *(KEHR uh tihn),* which is the same material that human fingernails and toenails are made of. Trimming a horse's hoofs and nailing shoes to them does not hurt any more than cutting our own nails, and it actually spares the horse a lot of pain from injuries and hoof diseases.

A farrier shoeing
a horse

# What About Training a Horse?

Training a horse takes skill and patience. Ideally, it should begin when the animal is a foal, which is a horse that is younger than 1 year old. A trainer must get a foal used to a halter. A halter is a leather or nylon device that fits around the horse's head and attaches to a lead rope (a rope used for leading the horse). After the horse is 1 year old, a trainer gradually gets the horse used to having a saddle on its back. Then the trainer can get on the horse's back and ride the animal for a few steps. Rides get longer as the horse gets used to being ridden.

After the horse has learned to follow the basic signals of a rider, such as stop, go, and slow down, it can be trained for certain sports. These sports might include racing; dressage *(dreh SAZH),* in which a rider guides a horse through various paces and movements without using reins or noticeable signals; or show jumping, an exhibition of skill in riding a horse over various obstacles.

Lipizzan horses during a training session

27

# What Kinds of Exercise or Play Are Needed?

The amount of exercise an Arabian horse needs depends on where it lives. An Arabian that lives in a stall needs daily riding exercise and a chance to run on its own in an enclosed area. An Arabian that lives in a paddock (see page 18) might not need to be taken out for extra exercise every day, but it should be ridden at least three or four times a week. An Arabian that lives in a pasture has enough space to get the free exercise it needs, but it still needs to be ridden regularly.

Another form of exercise for a horse is called lungeing. With this maneuver, a person stands in the middle of an imaginary circle with the horse on a rope around 30 feet (9 meters) long; the horse moves around the circle at a walk, trot, or canter.

Some Arabians love to play with toys. One favorite is a "jolly ball," a large plastic ball with a handle the horse can grip in its mouth.

Arabian mares
and their foals

29

# How Can You Help a Horse Care for Its Young?

It is important to provide the mare with a clean area to give birth and to be with her newborn. Infection is the biggest risk to a newborn foal, and many infections can be avoided by keeping the birthing area clean and disinfected.

A mare can often give birth to and care for a newborn foal without much help from humans. But, if needed, the foal can be rubbed briskly with clean straw or a towel, if the mare permits it. Make sure the foal nurses within the first two to three hours of its life. If the foal is weak and unable to stand, it may need help.

Have both mare and foal examined by a veterinarian immediately after the foal's birth. Then, carefully monitor the newborn foal for the first few days of its life. A healthy foal should become stronger and more active during this time. Increased time spent lying down or sleepiness may be signs of serious trouble in a foal—call a vet.

Helping a foal to nurse

# Are Horses Loners?

Horses are social animals, not loners. In the wild, they have a strong instinct to belong to a herd. In the herd, they are part of a hierarchy *(HY uh RAHR kee),* which is a group arranged in higher and lower ranks. In a herd, horses are protected from animals that might prey, or feed, upon them. The leader of the herd also leads the horses to food and water.

Whenever two horses meet, they "greet" one another. First, they stretch out their heads and sniff each other's noses, then they smell other parts of the body. Horses may shove and press against each other, lay their heads on each other's backs, and touch noses again. The greeting helps the horses to get acquainted, to recognize one another by their scents, to communicate their social status, and maybe even to test their strength.

A domesticated horse may feel it is either above or below a human, but it rarely feels it is the human's equal. Even though a horse isn't part of a herd, if a horse sees its owner as its "leader," it will look to that owner for directions when it is scared or anxious.

32

Horses greet
one another

33

# What Are Some Other Types of Light Horses?

In addition to the Arabian, the light horse group includes the Tennessee walking horse, the Morgan, and the quarter horse.

The Tennessee walking horse was bred to be comfortable to ride. These horses are especially noted for their comfortable walk and smooth canter (see page 52).

Morgan horses can be traced back to a New England stallion named Justin Morgan. These horses were originally used as harness horses.

Quarter horses were developed in North America during the early 1700's. Breeders crossed thoroughbreds (see page 38) from England with horses from the Spanish colonies of North America. The new breed could start quickly and run at high speeds for short distances. Cowhands use quarter horses for cutting—that is, selecting out certain cattle from a herd—and for other kinds of ranch work. Quarter horses can start, stop, and turn quickly, so they are are well suited for this work.

34

A quarter horse
working on a ranch

# Are Light Horses Also Grouped by Color?

Light horses are sometimes grouped according to color instead of by breed. Such groupings include palominos and albinos.

Breeders in the United States and Mexico developed the palomino line. Palominos have a golden coat and a light blond or silvery mane and tail. Most palominos have white only on the face and on the lower legs. Almost every breed except the thoroughbred has some horses with palomino coloring. A palomino mare and stallion often produce a foal of another color.

A true albino is an animal that, because of heredity, has no color in its eyes, hair, or skin. Its offspring also lack color. Some horse breeders, however, use the word albino to describe any horse with a white or pale-colored coat. But, these albino horses are not true albinos, as they all have some color that their offspring can inherit. One kind of horse called an albino has a pink skin, ivory coat, white mane, and blue eyes. Another kind has pink skin, a white coat, and brown eyes.

An Arabian with palomino coloring

# What Is a Thoroughbred?

One breed that developed from the Arabian horse is the thoroughbred.

All thoroughbred horses can be traced back to three Arabian stallions named the Byerly Turk, the Darley Arabian, and the Godolphin Arabian (sometimes called the Godolphin Barb). The three horses probably originated in the Middle East and were brought to England in the late 1600's and early 1700's. They were mated with English mares in an attempt to produce superior race horses.

Before the end of the 1700's, the English had developed a new breed of race horse called the thoroughbred. The breed displayed a remarkable ability to carry weight over longer distances with sustained speed.

Thoroughbreds are high-spirited, sensitive horses. They have powerful lungs and long, muscular legs, which make them especially well suited for racing. They are also used for jumping and hunting. Many polo ponies are part thoroughbred.

A thoroughbred mare
and her foal

# What Are Some Types of Heavy Horses?

Heavy horses can be divided into heavy harness horses and draft horses.

Heavy harness horses, which are also called coach horses, were bred to pull coaches, wagons, and artillery (mounted guns, such as cannons). These horses weigh less than draft horses and are not as strong.

Draft horses are the tallest, heaviest, and strongest group of horses. They are descended from the war horses that armored knights rode into battle. Draft horses once pulled plows on farms and hauled freight wagons from town to town. Draft breeds include the Clydesdale and the Belgian.

The Clydesdale, one of the most handsome draft breeds, has long, flowing hair—called feathers—below the knee and the hock (the joint on the hind legs).

The Belgian ranks among the strongest of heavy horses. Heavy muscles give the Belgian a stout appearance, and its head may look too small for its huge body.

Clydesdales

41

# What Are Some Types of Ponies?

Pony breeds include the Welsh, Hackney, and Connemara. Each of these breeds has different strengths. Miners in Wales developed the Welsh pony to work in the cramped tunnels of coal mines. The Hackney pony, developed in England, is a breed of larger sized ponies used to pull carriages. The Irish Connemara pony is known for its ability to jump.

A favorite pony breed is the Shetland. This breed once pulled plows and wagons in its native Shetland Islands, which are part of Scotland. Early Shetland ponies had thick bodies and legs. Some Shetland ponies have retained the powerful build of the original Shetland ponies. Others have been crossbred with lighter ponies to produce animals with more slender and graceful features. All Shetlands have thick manes and tails. Most are black or brown. A full-grown Shetland pony stands from 32 to 46 inches (81 to 117 centimeters) high.

Welsh ponies

43

# Are Horses Smart?

Horses are able to do certain types of thinking. For example, a horse is able to figure out how to open the bolt on a stable door or on a gate. Researchers have also shown that horses are able to classify objects (arrange objects into groups by type).

Horses are usually eager to please their owners or trainers, and most horses can be trained to obey commands. A horse may learn to come to its owner, for example, when the owner whistles. A horse can also be trained to do such things as take a "bow" when its trainer gives a signal.

In fact, horses can learn to respond to even the slightest signals. People who watch an expert rider on a well-trained horse often cannot see these signs. For example, the horse might move forward when the rider's legs are pressed lightly against the horse's side. Or, the horse might turn at a touch of the reins and a rider's leg.

44

A Lipizzan horse
taking a bow

# What Is Horse Sense?

Horse sense is a term people use to mean "common sense." It may be that some horses have horse sense, but all horses have physical senses that they use to tell what is happening in their world.

One kind of sense a horse uses is its vision. A horse's eyes are oval and are set on the sides of its head. The two eyes can be moved independently, each in a half circle. A horse, therefore, can look forward with one eye and backward with the other.

Horses have a well-developed sense of smell. Their nostrils are very large and can pick up scents from far away. Strong wind and heavy rain interfere with their sense of smell and may cause horses to become nervous. A horse uses its sense of smell, along with its vision, to identify people and other horses. A mare identifies her foal by its smell. The foal can also recognize the scent of its mother.

Horses have keen hearing. They have short, pointed ears that they can move around to pick up sounds from almost any direction. Horses can detect sounds above and below the range of sounds that humans can hear.

46

An alert horse uses its senses to learn about its environment

# How Do Horses Communicate?

Horses make a variety of sounds, including neighing, whinnying, nickering, squealing, and grunting. These sounds can express a range of emotions. A short whinny is usually a warning call, and a long whinny is an expression of contentment.

Horses also use their bodies to communicate their emotions and moods. This is called body language. For example, before a fight, a horse may stamp the ground with a front foot or rear up on its hind legs.

Other forms of body language include the head and tail. When a horse has its ears pinned back and it reaches its head toward you, it's sending the message, "Stay back or I may bite you." When it has its ears forward and its head held high, it may be wondering, "What is this object in front of me?" When a horse swishes its tail, it may be communicating that it is irritated or feeling ill. In the stable, pawing the ground with front feet may be the horse's way of sending the message that "I want to go out."

48

Horses displaying
body language that
precedes a fight

49

# What Are a Horse's "Blind Spots"?

A horse can see about 350 degrees—nearly a complete circle—around from its nose because its eyes are positioned on the sides of its head. By comparison, dogs can see only about 240 degrees around, and cats have only a 200-degree field of view. Nonetheless, a horse has some "blind spots," or areas that it cannot see. These areas include:

- The area directly in front of its forehead, extending for about 4 feet (1.2 meters). Never approach a horse directly from the front— if you do so, it can't see you until you are about 6 inches (15 centimeters) from its face.

- The area directly under its head on the ground and near its front legs. A horse can't see its own knees and chest.

- The area of its back directly behind its head.

- The area directly behind its tail. This is the most important blind spot to be aware of; if a horse becomes frightened, it could kick and hurt you. Be careful and alert when you walk behind a horse.

50

A woman stands where her horse can see her

# What Are Gaits?

Gaits are the ways that a horse moves as it walks or runs. Horses have four gaits that are natural to them, which they do not need to be taught: walk, trot, canter, and gallop.

Walk

A walk is the slowest gait. The horse moves at about 4 miles (6 kilometers) an hour. In a walk, a horse's right back foot strikes the ground; then its right front foot strikes the ground; its left back foot, and finally its left front foot. Each step takes place over one beat, so the walk is a four-beat gait.

A trot is a two-beat gait at about 9 miles (14 kilometers) an hour. On the first beat, the horse's right front and left back foot strike the ground. On the second beat, its left front and right back foot strike the ground.

Trot

A canter is a three-beat riding gait. A horse canters at 10 to 12 miles (16 to 19 kilometers) an hour. On the first beat, one back foot strikes the ground. (Some horses begin a canter with their left back foot and others with their right back foot.)

A horse galloping

Canter

On the second beat, the other back foot and opposite front foot hit the ground together. On the third beat, the other front foot strikes the ground.

A gallop is a horse's fastest natural gait. It consists of four beats. For the first two beats, the back feet strike the ground one after the other. On the third and fourth beats, the front feet hit the ground in the same order as the hind feet did. Then the horse leaps forward, and all its feet leave the ground

Gallop

# What Is a Horse Show Like?

Horse shows give you a chance to demonstrate your skill as a rider and trainer, as well as your horse's breeding and ability. Most shows are sponsored by a breed or performance association or local horse group.

Shows can be grouped into three categories: (1) performance, (2) breeding, and (3) equitation *(EHK wuh TAY shuhn),* or horsemanship.

In a performance competition, the horses and riders demonstrate various skills. For example, a show may include jumping events or events in which a horse is meant to move with a specific gait (see page 52).

In a breeding competition, all of the horses in the event are of the same breed. The judges rank the horses based on which they feel best represent the physical type necessary for that breed.

In an equitation competition, the contestants ride their horses around a ring. Competitors are judged on how well they ride and control their horse.

54

Show jumping

# What Are Some Common Signs of Illness in Horses?

Signs of illness in a horse include loss of appetite, lack of vigor (active physical strength), mucous or bloody discharge from the eyes or nose, swellings or sores on the body, and hot legs or feet. A fast or slow breathing rate or pulse rate may also be a sign of illness. Normally, a resting horse breathes from 8 to 16 times per minute and has a pulse rate of from 30 to 40 beats per minute.

One of the most common medical complaints horses suffer is colic. Colic is pain in the horse's abdomen. It can be caused by a number of things, some very serious. Signs of colic can include sweating, loss of appetite, teeth grinding, rolling, looking at or kicking the flank, and depression. Colic can be fatal, so it must be treated promptly.

Other signs that a horse is ill can include a high temperature, flared nostrils, and poor blood flow to the gums. But any change in the condition or behavior of a horse can be a sign that the horse is not well. If you are worried about your horse's health, always call a veterinarian immediately.

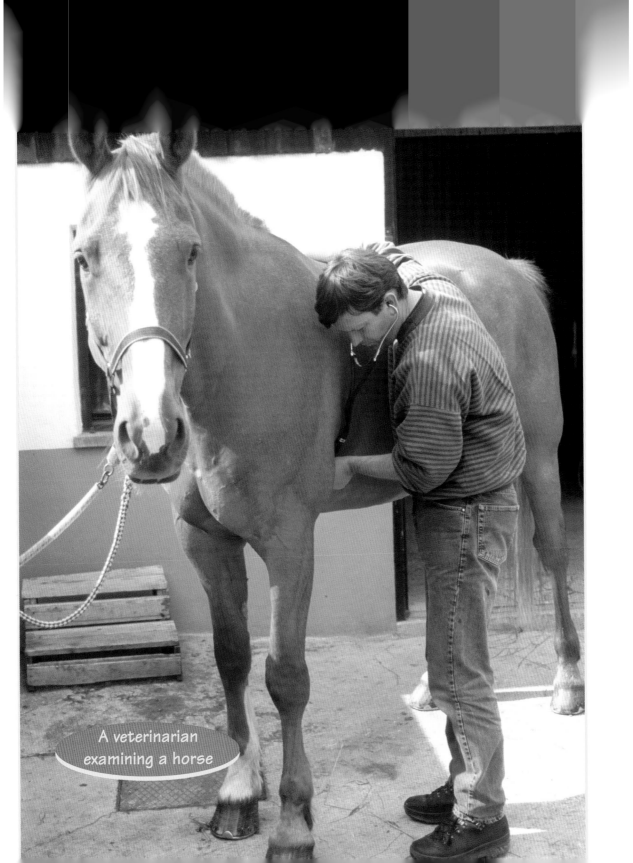

A veterinarian
examining a horse

# What Routine Veterinary Care Is Needed?

Routine veterinary care will help your horse live a long and healthy life. You should have your horse examined by a vet at least once or twice a year. One difference between medical care for horses and for other pets is that usually the horse vet will come to your animal rather than the other way around.

Horses need vaccinations against tetanus and influenza. Depending on where you live, your veterinarian may also suggest having your horse vaccinated for such diseases as rabies or West Nile virus. When needed, horses should receive medicine to expel worms (internal parasites).

Sometimes, a horse's teeth must be floated, or filed down, to remove sharp edges. Either a vet or an equine dentist can do this.

Most horses also need shoes. All horses should have their hoofs trimmed regularly. A registered farrier can perform this job.

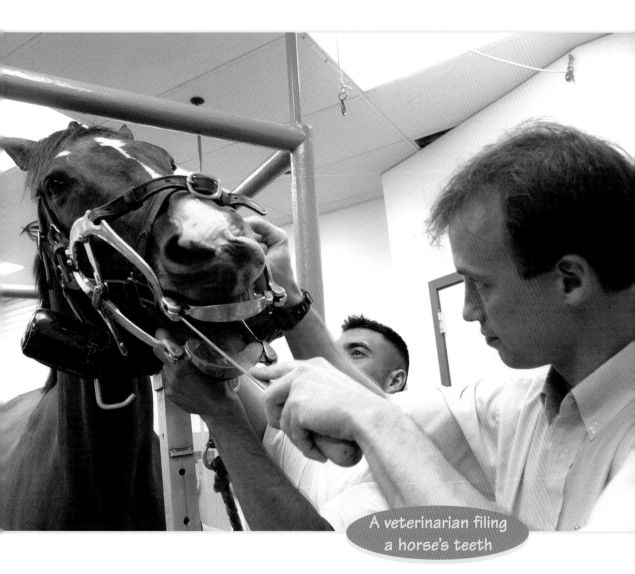

A veterinarian filing
a horse's teeth

59

# What Are Your Responsibilities as an Owner?

As an owner, you need to make sure that you:

- Feed and shelter your horse properly

- Keep your horse and its living quarters clean

- Exercise your horse regularly

- Groom your horse regularly

- Have your horse examined by a veterinarian at least once or twice a year

- Consult a vet if your horse appears to be ill

Owning a horse is a long-term commitment. Horses can live 25 to 30 years, or even longer. When you buy or adopt a horse, you must be sure that you can take care of it for that long. Otherwise, you must be prepared to find a new owner for the horse if the time comes when you can no longer give the animal the attention it deserves. A horse is a loyal companion and a dependable animal for riding, sport, and work, and it deserves your respect and care.

Feeding a horse

61

# Horse Fun Facts

→ The beloved children's book by Walter Farley, *The Black Stallion,* is about a half-wild Arabian horse.

→ Genghis Khan, Napoleon, Alexander the Great, and George Washington all rode Arabians.

→ The shire is the largest breed of horse. This breed developed in England after King Henry VIII had horses under 5 feet (1.5 meters) in height destroyed as useless.

→ Evidence suggests that chariot races were held in eastern Europe and northern Africa soon after the chariot was introduced there, in about 1500 B.C.

→ The record for the longest lived horse goes to the English horse Old Billy, who died at age 62 in 1822.

→ Horses never shed the hair of the mane or the tail.

→ Horses cannot vomit.

→ Race horses have their official birthday on January 1, except in countries of the Southern Hemisphere, where it is on either August 1 or July 1. Regardless of its actual birth date, a race horse becomes a year older on its official birthday.

# Glossary

**breed** To produce animals by carefully selecting and mating them for certain traits. Also, a group of animals having the same type of ancestors.

**currycomb** A comb or brush with metal teeth for rubbing and cleaning a horse.

**domesticated** A tame animal living with or under the care of humans.

**equine** About or having to do with horses.

**farrier** A blacksmith who shoes horses and trims their hoofs.

**foal** A horse that is younger than 1 year old.

**gait** Any one of the various manners of stepping or running of horses, such as the walk, trot, canter, or gallop.

**grooming** The act of rubbing down and brushing horses.

**hand** A unit of measure for horses that is equal to about 4 inches (10 centimeters).

**herbivorous** Feeding on grass or other plants.

**herd** A group of animals of one kind, especially large animals, that feed and travel together.

**heredity** The passing of physical or mental characteristics from one generation of animals to the next.

**mammal** A type of animal that feeds its young with milk made by the mother.

**mare** A female horse.

**parasite** An organism (living creature) that feeds on and lives on or in the body of another organism, often causing harm to the being on which it feeds.

**prey** Animals that are hunted and eaten by other animals. Also, to hunt or kill for food.

**stallion** A male horse.

**stride** The progressive movement of a horse, completed when all the feet are returned to the same position as at the beginning.

63

**For more information about Arabians and Other Horses, try these resources:**

*Complete Horse Care Manual*, by Colin Vogel, Gardners Books, 2005

*DK Horse & Pony Book*, by Carolyn Henderson, Dorling Kindersley, 2002

*Horse & Pony Care*, by Sandy Ransford, Kingfisher, Reprint edition, 2004

*Simplify Your Riding: Step-by-Step Techniques to Improve Your Riding Skills*, by Wendy Murdoch, Carriage House Publishing, 2004

http://www.firsthorse.com/links.htm
http://www.4husa.org/
http://www.horse-country.com/index.html
http://www.narha.org/
http://www.ponyclub.org/

# Horse Classification

Scientists classify animals by placing them into groups. The animal kingdom is a group that contains all the world's animals. Phylum, class, order, and family are smaller groups. Each phylum contains many classes. A class contains orders, an order contains families, and a family contains genuses. One or more species belong to each genus. Here is how the animals in this book fit into this system.

## Animals with backbones and their relatives (Phylum Chordata)
### Mammals (Class Mammalia)
#### Odd-toed Ungulates (Order Perissodactyla)

**Arabians and Other Horses (Family Equidae)**
> Genus *Equus*
>> Species *caballus*